NATU

More
Baby Wild
Animals

HERITAGE

Victoria | Vancouver | Calgary

Heritage House Publishing Company Ltd.
heritagehouse.ca

CATALOGUING INFORMATION AVAILABLE FROM LIBRARY AND ARCHIVES CANADA

978-1-77203-138-6 (pbk)

Cover design by Jacqui Thomas
Interior book design by Setareh Ashrafologholai
Cover photos by critterbiz/shutterstock.com (front) and AWenner/shutterstock.com (back)

Interior photos used by permission of the following, and obtained from **iStockphoto.com**:
Ray Hems [lion]; Norman Morin [armadillo]; Craig Dingle [swan]; Mark Weiss [rhinoceros]; Mark Kostich [snake];
Johannes Lodewlkus Van Der Merwe [buffalo]; StuPorts [hippopotamus]; victoriarak [squirrel]; John Pitcher [wolf];
Terry Wilson [deer]; Angelika Stern [chameleon]; italiansight [tortoise]; WLDavies [cheetah]; belizar73 [anteater];
Hung_Chung_Chih [panda]; Jeff McGraw [fox]; Christopher Meder [beluga]; Hailshadow [salmon]; KeithSzafranski [penguin];
Craig Dingle [peacock]; &#169 Kurt Hahn [moose]; draco-ziat [eagle]; OlenaShkatulo [seagull]; Aly Tyler [hedgehog];
and **Shutterstock.com**: Maggy Meyer [lion, title page]; Dean Bertoncelj [puma, page 3]; Monika Wieland [orca];
Don Mammoser [grizzly bear]; Mees Kuiper [giraffe]; David J Martin [seal]; Gerald A. DeBoer [raccoon]; uzuri [gorilla];
Vladimir Melnik [toucan]; photomatz [crow]; AWenner [elephant]; bikeriderlondon [great horned owl];
Zhiltsov Alexandr [tiger]; Beverly Speed [clownfish]; Orhan Cam [alligator]; Andrzej Kubik [zebra];
outdoorsman [porcupine]; apple2499 [koala]; Mertens Photography [monkey].

The interior of this book was produced using FSC-certified, acid-free paper,
processed chlorine free and printed with soy-based inks.

We acknowledge the financial support of the Government of Canada through
the Canada Book Fund (CBF) and the Canada Council for the Arts, and the Province of British
Columbia through the British Columbia Arts Council and the Book Publishing Tax Credit.

20 19 18 17 16 1 2 3 4 5

Printed in China

SOME wild animals are born totally helpless, just like human babies. They cannot walk or care for themselves, and they rely on their parents for everything. Other wild animals learn to walk, swim, fly, play, and fend for themselves days—or even hours!—after they are born! But all baby animals have a special connection with their parents, just like we do. This book has pictures of all sorts of baby animals living in the wild. Some live on land—in forests, jungles, or deserts—or in nests or burrows below the ground. Others live in the sea or on big icebergs. Still others live high up in trees and will later learn to fly through the sky. Some are really cute, and others might look a little bit icky or strange. But all baby animals are interesting in their own way!

LION

ORCA

GRIZZLY BEAR

ARMADILLO

SWAN

GIRAFFE

RHINOCEROS

SEAL

SNAKE

RACCOON

GORILLA

BUFFALO

TOUCAN

HIPPOPOTAMUS

CROW

WOLF

DEER

CHAMELEON

TORTOISE

CHEETAH

ANTEATER

PANDA

ELEPHANT

GREAT HORNED OWL

FOX

TIGER

BELUGA

SALMON

PENGUIN

PEACOCK

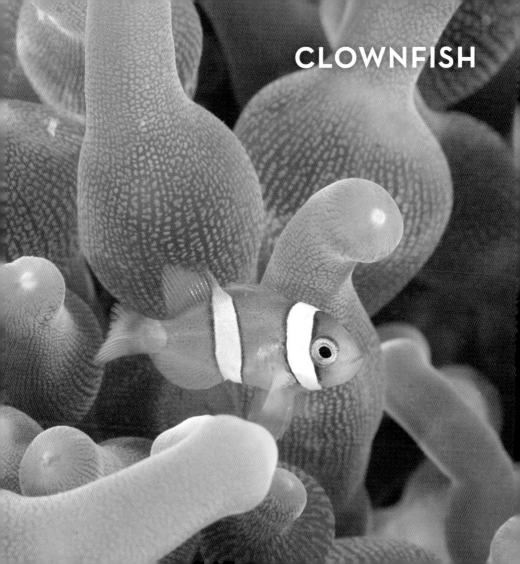

CLOWNFISH

ALLIGATOR

MOOSE

EAGLE

ZEBRA

PORCUPINE

KOALA

MONKEY

HEDGEHOG